In A Conning Tower Or How I Took H.M.S. Majestic Into Action: A Story Of Modern Ironclad Warfare

Hugh Oakeley Arnold-Forster

IN A CONNING TOWER;

OR,

HOW I TOOK H.M.S. "MAJESTIC" INTO ACTION.

A STORY OF MODERN IRONCLAD WARFARE.

BY

Hugh Oakley

H. O. ARNOLD-FORSTER.

Illustrated by

W. H. OVEREND.

Reprinted, by permission, from "Murray's Magazine."

CASSELL & COMPANY, LIMITED:

LONDON, PARIS & MELBOURNE.

1891.

"SWEPT AND SHATTERED BY THE POINT-BLANK DISCHARGE OF THE TERRIBLE ARTILLERY, THE 'MAJESTIC' STILL HELD HER COURSE" (*p.* 45).

PREFACE.

SOME explanation is required in placing this sketch in its present form before the public. The object of the writer has been to give a faithful idea of the possible course of an action between two modern ironclads availing themselves of all the weapons of offence and defence which an armoured ship at the present day possesses. An attempt has been made to throw into a popular form the teaching of various trials and experiments which have from time to time been made, and to introduce into the story of an actual engagement the results of a long course of careful observation of modern naval progress.

The point to which the greatest prominence has been given is the responsibility which must in the future attach to the officer commanding a battle-ship in action. The concentration of the whole complex machinery of a vessel in the hands of one man cannot fail to impose a strain upon the nerve and judgment of a commander, which only the strongest natures and coolest heads will be able to bear.

The element of chance which has always had its share in deciding the fate of battles will, however, not be less potent in the future than it has been in the past. Indeed, it is probable that the failure of a mechanical appliance, the accidental destruction of some essential machine, may neutralise in a moment the skill of a commander and the courage of his men. In the story that follows an attempt has been made to illustrate this danger by an example of such an occurrence.

Sailors will at once recognise the type of ship represented in the illustration as H.M.S. *Majestic.* She is a vessel similar in most respects to H.M.S. *Victoria.* It has been assumed, however, that the ship has been provided with the rapid-firing 6-inch guns which are probably destined before long to take the place of the ordinary service 6-inch breech-loader in the secondary batteries of all our large ironclads.

The author, though only an amateur student of naval matters, has endeavoured to make himself familiar with the conditions under which our modern ships must operate.

It is a source of great satisfaction to him to know that ample testimony has been borne by many naval officers to the accuracy of the story contained in these pages.

———

I am glad to be able to quote the following from among the many opinions which have been expressed with regard to the general accuracy of the description :—

"I bear witness to the accuracy of your sketch with great pleasure. There is nothing I have seen which comes so near the seaman's idea of what the future sea fight will be. I was much impressed by the article before I knew its authorship, and I have nothing but compliments for your handling of so difficult a subject."

From CAPTAIN CHADWICK,
Commanding U.S.S. *Yorktown,* formerly U.S. Naval
Attaché in London.

Extract from speech of Sir Nathaniel Barnaby, at the Institution of Naval Architects :—

"Some of us have read the very clever sketch of a naval engagement entitled 'In a Conning Tower.' The sudden destruction of the enemy's ship by the ram is not an unfair picture of what may happen even to a 14,000-ton ship."

SIR NATHANIEL BARNABY,
Late Chief Constructor of the Navy.

Lord Brassey, in the *Times*, writes :—

" The carnage which would occur in action at unprotected guns has been described with vivid imagination by the author of 'In a Conning Tower.'"

H. O. A.-F.

IN A CONNING TOWER;

OR,

HOW I TOOK H.M.S. "MAJESTIC" INTO ACTION.

HAVE you ever stood within a Conning Tower? No; then you have not set foot in a spot where the spirit of man has borne the fiercest and direst stress to which the fell ingenuity of the modern world has learnt to subject it. You have not seen the place where the individual wages a twofold contest with the power of the tempest and the violence of the enemy, where, controlling with a touch and guiding with his will the gigantic forces of Nature, he stands alone in the presence of death, and asserts amidst the awful crash of the mental and physical battle the splendid majesty of the spirit of man. For indeed there is nothing grander, more consoling to humanity, than the power of man to hold his own unshaken and unshakable in the face of unknown and incalculable dangers, upborne by the high inspiration of personal courage, by devotion to duty, or by the power of faith.

"Such a gift is vouchsafed to man"; but it is often

bought at a great price, and often, though life be spared to him who wins it, and though the human protagonist come out a victor in the contest, he survives with the scars of the terrible conflict burnt in for ever upon his inmost soul.

I have known a man, a giant in mind and body, emerge from the ordeal with hair blanched in an hour by the dread and strain of the conflict. Another I could tell you of, he who writes these lines, to whom the struggle between fear and duty, between terror and pride, brought the keenest suffering and the hardest trial which a man can bear.

Yes, I use the words fear and terror. I who have fought not without honour and success for my sovereign and my country, who bear on my breast the cross for valour, and whose name is not unknown among my countrymen and my comrades.

But let me come to the story I have to tell you. You have never set foot inside a Conning Tower. Let me do the honours of my old ship, and let me ask you to go with me on board H.M.S. *Majestic* as she lies at anchor at Spithead. There she floats, a heavy mass upon the water, ugly enough no doubt to an artist's eye, but with a certain combination of trimness and strength very grateful to a sailor, and especially to a sailor who knows every inch of her within and without, and whose duty it has been to make use of her terrible powers in war.

It is but a little way from the gig alongside on to the deck, and the ship in a bit of a sea is all awash where we stand. But we can take many a green sea on board the *Majestic* without being any the worse, and it takes a good deal to upset the equanimity of eleven[1] * thousand tons. Step through the door there. Stoop and raise your feet, for it is a strait gate. Now turn and look at the door you have passed. Talk of a banker's strong room, what banker in the world has a door like that; twelve inches of iron and steel, with a face that will turn all the " villainous centre-bits " that ever were forged ? But the door must needs be strong, for the treasure it has to keep behind it is the honour of the flag, and those who knock will come with a rat-tat equal to 60,000 tons on the square foot.[2] Now climb again : here we have more space, and things look more like the old man-of-war of the story books. Six guns on a broadside, and over a hundred men in the battery. Ah, when I think of that gun-deck as I saw it once ! You mark the racer of this after gun ; come forward now to No. 3 on the port side. All that is new work, a single shell ripped the battery side away for fifty feet from this point where you stand. Carriages, bulkheads, girders, beams, crumpled and torn like a tangle of bunch grass by an autumn gale.

* The numbers in the text refer to the Notes at the end of the book.

This is the spot to which I wish to lead you. This is
the Conning Tower of H.M.S. *Majestic.* A chamber scarce
six feet across, encumbered as you see with a score of
appliances which diminish the scanty space which it
affords. Touch the wall in front of you—a formidable
partition, is it not ? Twelve inches of solid steel and iron,
and carried down far into the framework of the ship.
Note too above your head a solid roof of steel. This is
the fighting position of the *Majestic.* "The fighting
position," you will say, "but how can an action be con-
ducted from a spot from which no enemy is visible ? "
Stand here and bring your eye to the level of the armour-
plating, and mark the narrow slit between the arched
cupola above us, and the steel walls of the chamber ;
sweep your eye round, and the whole horizon will come
within your view. Look down, and in front of you is the
sharp bow of the ship, and the two long white muzzles of
the guns protruding many feet from the forward turret.
Now look inside at the fittings of the Conning Tower, and
read the inscriptions on the brass tablets which surround
it. Over that group of speaking tubes on your right you
see the words, " Bow torpedo tube " and "above-water
torpedo tube." On the left is the voice tube to the
engine-room. That key completes the circuit which discharges the great guns.

Here in the centre is the steam steering-wheel, binnacle,

and compass. "All very trim and ship-shape," you will say, "and an immense convenience to the commanding officer to have all the arrangements of the ship brought under his hand."

Convenient, yes! but let your imagination come to the aid of your observation. Here lies the great ironclad, "a painted ship upon a painted ocean;" but see her as I have seen her; think, if you can, of what is meant by the accumulation of forces within this little space, and try to realise, as clearly as any man who has not passed through the ordeal can realise, the strain upon the human mind which is placed in absolute control of this mighty engine in the day of battle.

Every Englishman who is worth his salt knows something of the glorious naval annals of his country. The names of Rodney, Howe, and Nelson, are happily and rightly household words among us; we honour and revere those splendid masters of their art. Courage, skill, and a magnificent patriotism, were theirs. All that their country demanded of them they did. But compare for a moment the position of any one of those great officers in action, and that which the fearful ingenuity of modern science has imposed on their successors. On the one hand we have the Admiral standing on his quarterdeck, his star upon his breast, the central figure of his crew, animating them by his presence, and inspiring the group of officers who

B

stand around him with the spirit which his great example in previous victories has set them. By his side stands the Master; it is his business to sail and navigate the ship. The first lieutenant, charged with the discipline of the crew and the fighting of the guns, will see that there is no slackness, no want of skill in working the long tiers of the broadside carronades; an easy task, for it does not require either his vigilance or the example of his subordinates to strengthen the fierce rivalry between each gun's crew. Already the order has been passed that it is the duty of each ship to lay itself alongside of the enemy and to remain there till she has struck. The Master will lay the ship alongside, and the grimy gunners will continue to discharge their pieces at point-blank range[3] until the wooden wall of the opposing ship is battered into a shapeless mass of smoking timber, and until the joyful news comes from the deck that the enemy's ensign has sunk from the peak in token of submission.

That was in the olden time. What are the conditions of modern war?

Here in this spot is concentrated the whole power of the tremendous machine which we call an ironclad ship.

Such power was never since the world began concentrated under the direction of man, and all that power, the judgment to direct it, the will to apply it, the knowledge to utilise it, is placed in the hands of one man, and one only.

What is this power?

Talk of Jove with his thunderbolts, of Nasmyth with his hammer! the fables of mythology and the facts of latter-day science! where has there ever been anything to compare to it? Here in the Conning Tower stands the captain of the ship, and beneath his feet lie hidden powers which the mind can hardly grasp, but which one and all are made subservient to his will, and his will alone. Picture him as he stands at his post before the battle begins; all is quiet enough, there is scarcely a sound save the lapping of the water against the smooth white sides of the ironclad, and no outward sign of force save the ripple of the parted waters falling off on either side of the ram as it sheers through the water. But mark that white thread escaping from the steam-pipe astern, a fleecy vapour rising into the air and nothing more! But what does it mean? It means that far down below some thirty glowing furnaces are roaring under the blast of steam; that in the great cylindrical boilers the water is bubbling, surging, struggling, as the fierce burning gases pass through the flues; and that the prisoned steam, tearing and thrusting at the tough sides of the boilers, is already raising the valves and blowing off at a pressure of 100 pounds. It means that the captain in his Conning Tower has but to press the button by his side, and in a moment the four great engines will be driving the twin screws through the water with the force of 14,000 horse power,[4] and that the great ship, with the dead weight of 10,000 tons, will be rushing onwards at a speed of over twenty miles an hour.

In her turret and in her broadside batteries there is a deep hush of expectation; but there, too, waiting to respond to the "flash of the will that can," lie forces of destruction which appal the imagination.

Far down below our feet in the chambers of the great guns lie the dark masses of the powder charges. A touch, a spark, and in a sheet of flame and with the crash of thunder the steel shot will rush from their muzzles, speeding on their way 2,000 feet in a second, and dealing their blow with an impact of 60,000 foot-tons—5,000 pounds weight of metal,[5] discharged by one touch of the captain's hand. Nor is this all; another touch and another signal will liberate the little clips which detain the four Whitehead torpedoes in their tubes.[6] A puff of powder, a click, as the machinery is started and the two screws are set off whirling, and with a straight, silent plunge the long steel torpedoes will dive into the water, and at their appointed depth will speed on their way thirty miles an hour on their awful errand of destruction. Move that switch, and through the dark wall of the night a long straight beam will shoot forth with the radiance of 40,000 candles, turning the night into day.

A word spoken through that tube will let loose the

hailstorm of steel and lead from the quick-firing and
machine guns on the upper deck and in the tops. A discharge of shot and shell, not to be counted by tens or scores
but by hundreds and thousands, a storm before which no
living thing can stand, and under which all but the
strongest defences will wither and melt away like a snow-
bank under an April shower.

And last and most terrible of all, there is one other force
ready to the captain's hand: a force, the sum of all the
others, and which, if rightly utilised, is as irresistible as the
swelling of the ocean tide, or the hand of Death. By your
side and under your hand are the spokes of the steam
steering-wheel; far forward under the swirling wave, which
rises round the ship's cut-water, lies the ram, the most
terrible, the most fatal of all the engines of maritime warfare. It is the task of the hand which turns that little
wheel to guide and to direct the fearful impact of the
ram.

Think what the power confided to one man's hand
must be; 10,000 tons of dead weight driven forward by the
frantic energy of 14,000 horse-power, plunging and surging
along through the yielding waves, at a speed of ten feet in
every second, and with a momentum so huge that the
mathematical expression which purports to represent it to
the mind conveys no idea to an intelligence incapable of
appreciating a conception so vast. To receive a blow from

the ram is death, the irretrievable catastrophe of a ship's career. To deliver such a blow is certain victory. It is with the captain, and with the captain alone, as he stands here in the Conning Tower, that the responsibility of inflicting or encountering this awful fate lies.

Now you will understand what I mean when I say that never since the world began have such forces been placed in the hands of a single man, whose eye alone must see the opportunity, whose judgment alone must enable him to utilise it, and whose hand alone must give effect to all that his courage, his wisdom, and his duty prompt.

Perhaps you will ask what business have I, a naval officer, to allow such notions as these to run through my brain; what business have I to talk about anxiety or responsibility? The sailor's duty is plain; he has got to find the enemy, to fight him, and to beat him. If he be either fearful or anxious, he is a man out of place. But unfortunately naval officers are after all made of much the same stuff as other people; and there are certain circumstances in which their minds, however carefully tutored and prepared, are as much open to the strain of terror and anxiety as those of their comrades upon shore. Habit, personal courage, and a sense of duty, may enable them to overcome these enemies, but they feel their assaults. Do not believe a man when he tells you that he does not know what fear is on going into an action; above all, do not

believe it of the captain of a modern ironclad when about
to engage with an enemy of equal strength. True, he has
nothing to do but to carry out the duties which years of
practice have taught him how to perform; but the heart
never beat in a human frame whose pulsation was not
quickened by the presence of danger. Sit at home and
study the phenomena of electricity, codify the laws of the
elements, and analyse the progress of the lightning with a
Leyden jar and an electrometer, and you will doubtless
learn to contemplate the prospect of a thunderstorm with
a purely scientific interest. But stand alone in the night
on the mountain side, amid the roar and flash of a tropical
storm, and you must be either more or less than human if
your imagination and your spirit are not moved and awed
by the fierce play of Nature. And so it is with those
who in the time of battle have to command a ship of war.

By a piece of good fortune which had not fallen to the lot
of many of my colleagues, I had been two years in command
of my ship when the late war came upon us. I knew her, as
I have said, from stem to stern, from her armoured "top"
to her iron keel, and by day and by night, in my waking
hours and in my dreams, I had been going through every
conceivable form of engagement which my experience or
my imagination could suggest as likely to fall to the lot of
the *Majestic*. But sleeping or waking, by the light of
experience or by the light of fancy, I ever saw one

supreme moment when I should stand in this Conning
Tower, and should be called upon to take into my hand for
good or for ill, for success or failure, the mighty power of
the ship, and to make myself responsible for the honour of
the flag, the safety of the vessel, and the lives of the crew.

And always one great fact remained present to my
mind, that it was I, and I alone, who must do this thing;
that on *my* judgment, on *my* skill, on *my* courage, must
depend the issue of the day. I cannot describe to you how
deeply this feeling of responsibility weighed upon my spirit,
and how earnestly I prayed that when the time of trial
came I might be found worthy of the post I held.

Well! at last the time did come. Everybody knows
how strangely things were done at the outset of the war,
and everybody remembers the merciful escapes from
destruction, due not to forethought but to chance, which
enabled the country to survive the blunders and the
wanton carelessness of the Administration, and to live
through the first shock of the war. Luckily we all know
too, how, after chance had given us this happy and un-
deserved respite, the successes of our seamen, backed by
the energy of our constructors, enabled us to regain and to
assert that mastery of the sea which we had so nearly lost.

It was in the earliest days of this happier period, when
the need for organisation and system had begun to dawn
upon the official mind, but before much had been done

to give effect to the newly-awakened conviction, that the *Majestic* was ordered to join the Mediterranean fleet.

We steamed out of Portsmouth Harbour alone. It was a mad thing, and everybody knew it.

It was an axiom which every one of the gentlemen at Whitehall had long ago committed himself to on paper, that no heavy ironclad should go to sea in time of war without an attendant squadron of cruisers, despatch vessels, and torpedo-boats. But beggars must not be choosers; there was urgent need for my ship in the Mediterranean, and all our cruisers, despatch vessels, and torpedo-boats had too much to do in performing the immediate duties which the stress of the situation and the want of any reasonable organisation had forced upon them to allow of their attending the *Majestic* on her southward journey.

It is not easy to describe my feelings when our sailing orders arrived ; the mingled sensations which passed through my brain would be hard to analyse. At last the moment had come when the supreme ambition of my life was to be realised, and I was to command one of Her Majesty's ships in actual war. At the same time the total want of any experience to guide me in the enterprise which it was now my duty to undertake, and the feeling of uncertainty as to the correctness of the theories which my studies in peace time had led me to form, weighed upon my spirit to a painful degree. I must admit, however, that as we passed

the Warner Light,[7] and I telegraphed "full speed ahead,"
my feeling was one of extraordinary exhilaration. It is not
easy to describe the mental atmosphere which seemed to
pervade the ship; but one characteristic struck me as being
of good omen, and that was the feeling of cheerfulness
and good fellowship which appeared to animate all ranks of
the ship's company.

One odd incident I remember as peculiar to myself. I
had fully determined before I left port that I would dis-
mantle my cabin of all the pretty knick-knacks and
ornaments of which I was so proud, and which made it so
charming and comfortable a retreat. When, however, the
actual moment came for carrying my intention into effect,
I felt an indescribable reluctance to give the necessary
orders, and in the end I went to sea with scarcely a visible
alteration having been effected in the arrangements of my
cabin. The contrast between the pretty and homelike
surroundings in which I studied once more my plan of
action, and the terrible realities of the situation with which
I might at any moment find myself face to face, dwells
with a singular distinctness in my memory.

Our object being to reach Gibraltar unmolested and in
good fighting trim, we naturally gave the shore a wide
offing.

We had passed the Lizard Light some two hours when
we came in contact with the first evidences that the ocean

"WE FELL IN WITH H.M.S. 'SHANNON' SLOWLY MAKING HER WAY HOMEWARDS, AND BEARING PLAIN MARKS OF THE STRIFE IN WHICH SHE HAD BEEN ENGAGED" (*p.* 25).

had become the scene of a bloody and fatal conflict. It was at this point that we fell in with H.M.S. *Shannon* slowly making her way homewards, and bearing plain marks of the strife in which she had been engaged. We exchanged signals with her, but she reported that she had not seen an enemy's ship for forty-eight hours. It was not till long afterwards that we learnt the particulars of the engagement from which she had just emerged. How, over-taken by a protected cruiser, she had lost no less than eighty men in the vain attempt to work her broadside guns; how, preserved from destruction by her armoured belt, she had maintained herself until, by a lucky discharge, of the new 9-inch B.L. gun, which the Admiralty, in a fit of unwonted prescience, had placed in the bows, she had succeeded in exploding a heavy shell in a vital part of the enemy's ship; how, safe from pursuit, but with her crew decimated and her armour in splinters, she had made her way back to Plymouth : a testimony to the gallantry of her crew and to the error of her designers.[8]

It was two o'clock on the following day that the look-out sighted a strange vessel hull down on the port bow. It was not long before the diminished distance between the two vessels revealed to us the three funnels and the raking masts of one of the enemy's fast cruisers. A good glass enabled us to detect two torpedo-boats steaming along under her quarter. I knew at once what our friend was about, and I longed for a swift companion whom I might despatch in pursuit; but such good fortune was not to be. After making a careful inspection of us, the stranger went about, and, steaming at full speed, was soon beyond the horizon. To follow her was impossible, nor would it have been consistent with my instructions had I possessed the three extra knots which would have put me on an equality with her; but I was pretty sure, and the event proved that I was right, that she had not paid us her visit of inspection for nothing.

During the whole of the following night we were steering west-south-west, and our object in keeping so far from the land had been fulfilled, for we had sighted nothing but a homeward-bound British steamer from Valparaiso, which had made a clear run at an average rate of sixteen knots, and had not been molested by any enemy.

It was just after seven bells in the morning watch that the look-out man on the top signalled a vessel hull down on the port bow. It was a fairly bright morning, and the distance, as far as we could calculate, between ourselves and the vessel in question was about twelve miles.

Whoever the stranger might prove to be, there was little necessity for any extra precaution on board the *Majestic*. Throughout the night the water-tight doors had been closed; all movable bulkheads and unnecessary fittings had long ago been removed and stowed. Every man knew his station, and there was not the slightest occasion to hurry the men over their breakfast; the only difficulty was to keep them from their fighting stations, or from any point from which a view of the stranger could be obtained. In a very few minutes it became apparent that, whether friend or foe, the new-comer was heading directly for us. Our orders were not to seek an engagement; in this case it was evident that we should scarcely have an opportunity of refusing one, provided that we held our course, and that it was an enemy's ship that was in sight.

We were not long in doubt upon this head. In less than ten minutes not only the form but the colours of the stranger became clearly apparent, and the colours were those which it was our duty at any cost to lower.* The ship itself was as familiar to me as the flag which she bore. In these days, when photography and an elaborate professional literature have recorded the form and peculiarity of every important ship-of-war afloat, it would have been strange had I not recognised the formidable lines of the antagonist with which we were so soon to be in conflict.

* We learnt subsequently that the ironclad had been attended by the cruiser and torpedo-boats which we had seen on the previous day. Her auxiliaries had remained in port to coal, with orders to follow at speed in a few hours. Happily on leaving port they had been picked up by H.M. ships *Blenheim* and *Cossack*,[9] which after a running fight of an hour and a half had sunk the torpedo-boats and captured the cruiser.

But my acquaintance with my adversary was a more intimate one than any which the study of books could have conferred. It was not three months since I had been on board of her. Nor was this all; not only did I know the ship, but I knew who was in command of her. Many a time had I met Captain C—— when he represented his country as Naval Attaché in London. A more gallant officer, a more accomplished gentleman, never wore the uniform of the honourable service to which he belonged.

I confess that, when I first realised who was my opponent, a sensation of a very peculiar kind passed through my brain. On the one hand, feeling as I did perfect confidence in my ship and in my crew, and rejoicing, as every man in my position would have done, at this opportunity of performing the highest duty of my profession, I was gratified that my opponent was a man whose defeat must add a special lustre to the efforts of my crew if they should be successful. On the other hand I felt, as I stood on the bridge as the two ships neared each other, that the conflict must inevitably be not merely between material appliances on either side, but between the brain and the heart of two men whose fortunes and whose reputations were equally at stake; and I knew that the great ship that was bearing down upon us was guided by a master-mind, which would be quick to seize an opportunity, ready to strike, and merciless to gain victory at any cost. It was to

be a battle, no doubt, but it was also to be a duel, and a
duel to the death.

In less than half an hour from first sighting the enemy,
the distance between us was reduced to a little over two
miles. *(*a*) The crew were at their quarters,
the guns were loaded, the torpedoes were
charged and ready for action, and the boilers
were blowing off at their highest pressure:
for it had always been my fixed determination
to fight an engagement at full speed. Up to
this time I was standing close to the chart
house on the upper bridge; perhaps not the
wisest place to have selected, but I was determined to avail myself as long as possible of
the full power to sweep the horizon which
my entry into my appointed station in the
Conning Tower would so inevitably curtail. It
was hard at such a moment to believe that
the peaceful aspect before us must be changed
before we were many minutes older into a
hideous tempest of fire and blood. Many of
us on both sides had served our respective
countries for many years, but there was not
one of us to whom the circumstances of the

* The letters refer to the positions of the ships as shown in the
diagram.

C

approaching battle were not absolutely new and beyond
experience. The ship was making 105 revolutions, and
was running at a very high speed, over seventeen knots;
but the only sound was the crash of the engines, as familiar
to us as the very pulsation of our own hearts, and scarcely
more noticed. By my side stood two of my subordinates,
my. gunnery and navigating officers, my signalman and one
of his staff. The time for conversation had gone by; we
had said all that had to be said, but one more remark
remained to be made.

"Captain Maitland,"[10] I said to the staff-commander; "I
shall not require your services; this will be a matter of tactics,
and not of navigation; we may be in need of officers before
the day is out. I must ask you to leave the bridge; I
know you will regret it, but the interests of the service
demand it."

The words were scarcely out of my mouth, and the
officer had hardly left the ladder, when a tongue of flame
shot forth from the forward barbette of the enemy, and a
thick, eddying bank of white smoke rolled and tumbled
over her bows, driven forward by the blast of the great
gun. There was a pause, short enough indeed in our
ordinary reckoning of time, but fully long enough for
anxious and excited nerves to appreciate, ere the hostile
message reached its destination. Suddenly, some twenty
yards ahead of the *Majestic*, there rose into the air a vast

column of water, and the eye, naturally following the
direction of the shot, marked the great jets which sprang
up far into the distance as the projectile ricocheted over
the water.

The action had begun, and sooner than I had expected.
The range was a long one—too long to my thinking—but
evidently the enemy was not of the same opinion. The
time had come when duty demanded that I should take
my appointed station. I descended to the Conning Tower,
followed by my subordinates. As I passed down the
ladder, I saw the men duly posted at their stations in the
tops and on the superstructure, in charge of the quick-
firing guns. In the battery the larger quick-firing guns
were loaded and ready. Nothing was wanted in that part
of the preparations which my eye could reach, and I had
the happy certainty that there was no detail in all the
dark recesses of the ship which required vigilance and
skill for its superintendence which had not been cared for
by my officers.

A strange thrill came over me as I entered the Conning
Tower. No one can analyse the sensations of such a
moment; but one feeling I recall with pleasure and grati-
tude. Whether it were due to the happy inheritance of that
English temperament and those English traditions which
will reveal themselves in the time of danger, even to those
who have been least conscious of enjoying the advantages

they confer, whether it were the overmastering interest of the situation itself, and the professional instinct which compelled me to regard the whole proceeding as a problem of absorbing interest, I cannot say; but of this I am certain, that from that moment the feeling of doubt and anxiety, which I must admit had been for many hours past one of the sensations of which my mind was most deeply conscious, passed away, and was replaced by a feeling of mental exaltation, and of keen and almost oppressive appreciation of the conditions of the fight. However, I had little time at the moment to consider my sensations. I at once requested Lieutenant Mannering to communicate my orders with regard to laying the two heavy guns in the forward turret, and a general instruction was passed to the guns in the battery to reserve their fire until special orders were received from me. By this time the ships were within 2,000 yards of each other, the enemy about two points on our port bow. (*b*) Again I saw the bright flash spring from her sides, and in a moment it was followed by a shock which shook the *Majestic* from stem to stern. This time there was no error in the aim, and the steel shot had struck the ship on the thick plating abaft the turret. Subsequent examination showed a scar six inches deep; but the blow had been a slanting one, and the projectile flew off at an angle, and passed into the sea astern of us.

The time had come to give as good as we got. We were not near enough as yet to allow of the guns being successfully laid by my direction, and I passed the word down to bring both the turret guns to bear upon the enemy, and to fire as soon as she came on the sights. With a roar and with a crash which shook the tower in which I stood, the monster guns spoke their first word in war. Neither in the Conning Tower nor on the upper deck could the result of the shot be seen, but the signalman in the top gave us the welcome news that one shot at any rate had gone home. The guns' crews immediately commenced reloading, and looking through the slit of the tower I watched with intense anxiety the course of the enemy. There was a discharge from her decks, and in an instant there burst forth in front of my face, in all appearance on the very bow of the *Majestic*, a sheet of flame, followed by a crack like the rending of the thundercloud. At the same moment, with a din such as I had never heard in such close proximity, the broken fragments of the bursting shell beat down upon deck, on turret, on Conning Tower. The destruction was instantaneous, and within a certain area it was complete. Stanchions, bollards, bulwarks—the deck itself—were ripped and torn like so much paper; but the solid face of the turret held its own with ease, and the muzzles of the guns, to my immense satisfaction, remained untouched.

A second shot was more disastrous, striking the battery on the port side about half-way down its length ; it passed through the iron skin as through a gossamer, and bursting against the after bulkhead, spread ruin and death through the crowded space.   Never had a single shot worked more havoc, never did men recover themselves under such a stress with such coolness and bravery as did the survivors in the battery of the *Majestic*.[11]   I had deep reason to congratulate myself upon the order which I had previously given, that the guns' crews on the starboard side should go below until their guns could actually be brought to bear. But for this order the carnage would have been terribly increased.   Meanwhile my gunners were not idle, and the great guns had again tried the thickness of the enemy's sides, this time firing chilled shell, which proved by their detonation that they had found an obstacle.[12]

It was now the crisis of the battle, for I saw the enemy rapidly changing course, and, porting her helm, make a circuit which would soon bring her broad on our port beam. (c) Two courses were open to me: one was to hold on, to accept the encounter and run past at close quarters, exchanging fire on the beam ; but a moment's consideration convinced me that to do so would be to favour the manœuvre which my adversary had commenced, and which I had anticipated from the outset.   Once abaft my beam, his after-barbette guns would be as serviceable for attack

"A SECOND SHOT . . . SPREAD RUIN AND DEATH THROUGH THE CROWDED SPACE" (*p.* 34).

as his forward guns had already proved themselves to be. I was, unluckily, not in the same plight; my single stern gun was not of a calibre to engage singly against such odds.[13] At any cost I must keep my turret bearing on the foe. The alternative course therefore alone remained open to me.

I knew the turning circle of my ship to a yard, and in an instant I determined what to do.

The two ships were now in a blaze from stem to stern, the tops, the superstructure and the batteries in sheets of flame; my own fire, alas! diminished by the fatal shell which had played such havoc in my main battery.

Suddenly I saw that the time had come. The enemy was already heading in towards us, and in another moment his starboard guns would have opened upon us. Suddenly I gave the order " starboard, hard-a-starboard."[14] The order was executed as soon as given, and the splendid ship, answering to the helm, came round with a swift, steady rush that made my heart leap for joy. We were within three hundred yards, and with our starboard bow presented (*d*) to the enemy we rapidly approached to an even closer and more perilous range. The fire from the tops and superstructure had now slackened, for we had realised with sorrowful certainty the truth which modern warfare has revealed to us, that no exposed crew can live under the close fire of machine-guns. The loss on either side had

been terrific for so short an engagement, and mere physical
inability to load and work the guns had for a time caused
the fire to slacken. It was not my intention that the ship
should complete the half circle, and suddenly porting the
helm I bore down diagonally on the starboard quarter of
the enemy.

It was at this moment that both my antagonist and
myself resorted to another of the great weapons of destruction that had been confided to us, but which had not as
yet been called into play. I had given a general instruction to the officers in charge of the torpedo-tubes to
exercise their discretion in discharging their weapons as
soon as I informed them that a suitable stage in the operations had been reached. I now gave the required signal,
and it was at this moment, as I was subsequently informed,
that the starboard Whitehead was discharged. Almost at
the same instant, one of the few observers left in the top, a
midshipman who had found his way up there since the
machine-gun fire had slackened, noted that a similar step
had been taken by the enemy. I need hardly say that I
was unable myself to observe either of the incidents which
I have just related; the position of the Conning Tower, the
thickness of the smoke, and, above all, my intense preoccupation, prevented my appreciating the danger to which
at that moment my ship was exposed. By a fortunate
chance, however, an action of mine beyond all doubt

averted the peril which I did not myself foresee. The discharge of the torpedoes on either side was evidently almost coincident with my sudden alteration of course.

The *Majestic*, which a few moments before had been almost broad on the enemy's beam, had yielded to the pressure of the rudder and was already heading obliquely towards the other ship. (*e*) Our own torpedo, running with an accuracy and speed which left nothing to be desired, passed close under the stern of our adversary. The chance which diverted our attack proved also our protection.

The midshipman marked the moment of the discharge of the enemy's torpedo, and his eye followed the line of bubbles as it advanced with furious speed in the direction of the *Majestic*. Against the Whitehead torpedo once fairly launched against an unprotected ship there is no defence; the track of the terrible projectile is plainly visible to the eye, but no power can avert its course or parry the fatal blow. Seething and hissing, the torpedo came nearer; if the ship steadies on this course she must inevitably be struck; the hand which controls her is in the Conning Tower, and he who directs it is all unconscious of what depends upon the next movement of the little wheel in front of him. But the ship is not yet round, the slight pressure on the spokes is maintained, the steam steering-engine passes it on with its full power to the rudder, and the ship steadily swings up to starboard. It is touch and go : the hundredth part of a point less and the striker will come full against the bow of the ironclad, and the great problem of the value of the Whitehead torpedo in war will have been illustrated by a practical example which perhaps few of the ship's company will live to study. But no ! Hidden for a second under the curling swell above the ram, the hissing bubbles reappear, hastening away on our port bow, and this time, at any rate, the *Majestic* is saved.

But to return to my own immediate part in the engagement. The ship, whose course had been in the shape of an S, was now completing her second half-circle, and the guns trained over the beam were still bearing upon the enemy as she steamed away from us. (*f*) The starboard battery was remanned, and on both sides the firing was renewed with great vigour, though with a diminished accuracy which told that the loss of the leading men in the guns' crews and the fierce stress of the fight had produced their natural consequences. Suddenly, amidst the din of the firing, and easily distinguishable above the thunder of the guns, came the report of a fierce, rapid explosion, followed by an instantaneous cessation of the enemy's fire. It was impossible to see what had taken place, but the fact remained beyond doubt, and I instantly determined to avail myself of it. It had been my intention to have kept

L

"THE TRACK OF THE TERRIBLE PROJECTILE IS PLAINLY VISIBLE TO THE EYE" (*p.* 39).

my course at right angles to the enemy for a time, so that
I might steam out of torpedo range, and again take up an
end-on position. But this idea was instantly abandoned.
Once more the helm was put hard-a-port, and once more
the *Majestic* circled round on the further side of her
adversary. (*g*) In a moment firing was renewed, and the
enemy, to my surprise, came gradually round to port, as
though about to cross my bows. It is a source of unfailing
thankfulness to me to remember that at this crisis of the
battle my mind was cool and collected, and my judgment
perfectly clear. I turned to the lieutenant, and bade him
transmit my orders through the ship. The orders were
simple. " Lay both guns ahead, full speed and prepare to
ram."

I stood, with the steering-wheel in my hand, watching
every movement of the enemy; for a freshening breeze
now carried the smoke swiftly away. It was evident that
something of serious importance had taken place; her
speed was diminished, for the interval between the ships
decreased much more rapidly than the lateral distance.

I was convinced that for a time at any rate my
adversary had lost control over his ship. We were now
separated by a distance of less than three hundred yards,
(*h*) and still the same apparent indecision marked the
movement of the enemy, who was moving slowly with
almost a full broadside presented to us, and somewhat on

our starboard bow. Suddenly she appeared to gather full way, and her head began to come in slightly towards us. But it was too late; the time had come. I moved my hand and the officer by my side flashed my will to the great turret guns. On both sides there was a roar and a crash: the thunder of the tornado with the shock of the earthquake. So much I can recollect, but the next few moments remain a blank on my memory. I was stunned, but the loss of consciousness was only for a few instants. I recovered to find myself leaning against what had an instant before been the wall of the Conning Tower, but which now was but a fragment of the wreck with which everything around me seemed overwhelmed.

The view, which had hitherto been obscured by the low roof of the tower, was now open, for not only had the roof gone, but a huge piece of the solid wall of the tower itself had been caught by the impact of the great steel shot, and now lay in bent fragments and huge slabs on the iron deck below. Of the three who, a moment before, had stood together in the tower, I was the only survivor. My signal-man, crushed and mangled by the *débris* of the armour, lay in front of me. By my side my lieutenant had sunk down dead, his breast pierced by a single fragment of the flying metal. I raised my hand to my eyes to brush away the mist which I felt gathering upon them, and I found that my face was streaming with blood; but while reason was left to me, it could only be concentrated on one thought and one object: that which lay before me.

Swept and shattered by the point-blank discharge of the terrible artillery to which she had been exposed, the *Majestic* still held her course, and her course was that on which I had launched her. On either side the last bolt was sped, the gun had had its final word; a greater power was now to give its decision, and from that decision there was no appeal.

Those who attach any value to the humdrum division of time and distance by the ordinary standards of arithmetic and the clock-face, will doubtless be able to calculate for their own satisfaction that the period occupied in traversing two hundred and fifty yards at a speed of twenty miles an hour is to be reckoned in seconds only, and that the briefness of the allotted time gives no scope for the operations of the mind. Those who have ever stood in such a position as I stood in at that moment, will laugh at these dogmatic calculations, and will know as I know, that each second, and each portion of a second, is pregnant with its keen and separate consciousness.

The time, so heavily laden with the weight of the unknown result which it was about to . produce, crept heavily along. But the end came at last. To the last moment, from the high deck and superstructure of the enemy, the fire from the machine-guns was maintained

D

with a certain degree of energy. Our opponent lay
between us and the southern sun, and I can at this
moment remember the instant when the low bow of the
Majestic entered the shadow she cast upon the water.
Then with a deep, grinding, terrible crash, the ram did its
work. (*i*) We had struck the enemy about fifty feet from her
bow, and the slight change in her direction made the blow
a slanting one.

The *Majestic* shivered from stem to stern, and I could
actually see the ironwork on the bow ripping and splin-
tering as it forced its way into the opposing side. But it
was not there that the fatal wound had been given. Far
underneath the water-line the protruding ram had struck
a blow from which no human power could save the victim.
For a moment all was still, save for the sound of the
stretching and rending of the iron; then suddenly, with a
steady but certain heave, the great ship seemed to bow
down towards us. I watched her for a moment: long
enough to see the surface of the deck as it showed up with
the heel of the ship, and then I knew no more. The strain
was over, my work was done, and it was not till a month
later that I opened my eyes in Haslar hospital and came
back once more to the land of the living. Little remains
for me to tell, but you will ask how the two ships fared in
the encounter. Of the condition of my adversary I can
tell you but little, for no subsequent examination revealed

"THEN WITH A DEEP, GRINDING TERRIBLE CRASH, THE RAM DID ITS WORK" (*p.* 46).

the work of our guns. Within a quarter of an hour after
the ram of the *Majestic* struck her, the last vestige of the
splendid ship had sunk beneath the waves, her hull absolutely broken in two by the force of the collision. We had
time to save some hundred and twenty of her crew,* and
from them we learnt something of the effects of our
cannonade. A projectile from our forward turret had
struck one of a pair of barbette guns at four feet from the
muzzle. The chase [15] of the gun which was thus struck
had been broken clean away, and the gun alongside of it
had been so far dislodged from its slide that the loading
gear had become unserviceable. The rapid discharges of
the heavy quick-firing guns had been most destructive,
and it was to a hundred-pound shot from one of these
that the catastrophe, to which in all probability we owed
our victory, was due. Falling full upon the side of the
ship in the neighbourhood of the broadside torpedo discharge, the shot had carried a piece of the plate bodily
inwards ; and had come in contact with the striker of the
Whitehead torpedo, just as it was about to leave the
impulse tube.[16] An explosion had instantly followed, the
report of which we had heard, but of whose effects we had
no conception at the time. Seventy pounds of gun-cotton
exploding between decks had created havoc which might

---

* With the greatest difficulty, for we had not a single boat that would
swim, so destructive had been the effect of the machine-gun fire.

well appal the bravest. Nor was this all. The blast of
the explosion had driven a heavy piece of metal against
the connections of the steam steering-gear, and for a
moment all control over the movements of the ship had
been lost. Before the fatal moment, the ship was again in
hand; but it was too late, and the sequel has already been
told.

One other fact we were able to discover. The last discharge from our turret guns, at three hundred yards, had
gone home. One shot, piercing the armoured belt like
paper, had cut a passage through the ship almost from
stem to stern. The other, striking the Conning Tower, had
in an instant destroyed the gallant captain of the ship,
together with all those who stood round him.

On our side, with the exception of the final catastrophe,
the results had been no less terrible. The central battery,
torn as I have already pointed out by a heavy projectile,
had been riddled through and through by smaller shell
of every description. No less than ninety of our brave
fellows had fallen in this part of the ship in a courageous
attempt to keep up the fire of the broadside guns. In the
tops and on the superstructure our losses were only limited
by the number of men whom I had allowed to expose
themselves in those dangerous positions. On the superstructure not one man in ten escaped without a casualty
of some sort; but the thick walls of the turret had proved

an adequate protection.   With the exception of No. 1 of
the starboard gun, who had been struck dead by a
machine-gun bullet in the very act of aligning the sights,
not a single man of either gun's crew had been touched.
But the outside of the turret showed the terrible nature of
the attack to which it had been exposed.   On the port side
was a grazing dent ten inches in length, and scoring the
round surface of the turret for a yard or more.   A shell
exploding on the glacis plate had broken away the iron in
more than one place ; while, more remarkable than all the
other injuries was the spot where a salvo of five simul-
taneous or successive blows from the six-inch guns had
struck the steel-faced plating within the space of a square
yard.[17]

It was at this point that the armour had suffered most,
and the accumulated force of the attack had shivered the
metal, which, starred and cracked in every direction, had
fallen down in heavy fragments eight inches thick upon
the deck.

The last discharge of the heavy guns, which had well-
nigh proved fatal to me, had struck the *Majestic* in two
places.   The first shot, passing through the thin plating
at the bow like paper, had imbedded itself deep in the
forward bulkhead.   The second shot, striking the crown of
the Conning Tower, had carried away the iron roof and a
large portion of the wall of the structure.   Not a single

shot was fired during the whole of the action from our after gun. The blow of the ram which had annihilated our enemy had not seriously damaged the *Majestic.*[18] The strain had shaken and dislocated the plating round the bow, but the consequent leakage was well kept in check by the collision bulkhead, and was mastered by the steam-pumps. But our loss in men, in protection, and in ammunition, was too grave to allow of any alternative but a return into port, and the officer who succeeded me in command wisely decided upon adopting this course.

We returned to Portsmouth on the fifth day after leaving it. A single action, lasting less than thirty minutes, had decided the fate of two of the most powerful ships in the opposing navies.

As for myself, as I have told you, it was not till many days afterwards that I regained consciousness and learnt the facts which I have now recounted to you. During the weary period of my delirium, I acted over and over again every scene in the drama in which I had been recently engaged. Nor when the light of reason returned did the preoccupation pass from my mind, but from that time to this, and from now till the end of my life, the great crisis of my existence has ever been, and must ever be, the terrible time that I spent in the day of battle in the Conning Tower of H.M.S. *Majestic.*

NOTES.

[1] The displacement of H.M.S. *Victoria* is 10,470 tons.

[2] The muzzle energy of the 110-ton gun is 57,580 foot-tons.

[3] It is said that at Trafalgar the number one of the lower deck guns stood by with a bucket of water ready to dash into the hole made by the shot in the side of the enemy's ship, and thus to prevent an outbreak of fire.

[4] The total indicated horse-power of H.M.S. *Victoria* is 14,000 h.p. Estimated speed on measured mile, 16·75 knots.

[5] The total weight of the projectiles discharged from the heavy guns of H.M.S. *Victoria* is 5,300 lbs.

[6] In all modern torpedo tubes a small powder charge is used to propel the torpedo instead of compressed air.

[7] The Warner Light marks the entrance to Portsmouth Harbour.

[8] The construction of H.M.S. *Shannon* is very faulty; she has a 'thwart-ship armoured bulkhead, which is supposed to protect her crew from raking fire, but she has no side armour sufficiently high to protect the guns' crews. The broadside guns would practically be untenable under machine-gun fire. As a matter of fact, no such gun as that referred to has yet been supplied to H.M.S. *Shannon*.

[9] H.M.S. *Blenheim*, recently completed at the Thames Iron Works, is a fast protected cruiser of 9,000 tons, 20,000 horse-power, and with an estimated speed on the measured mile of 22 knots. She carries two 9·2-inch 22-ton, and ten 6-inch 5-ton breech-loading guns. H.M.S. *Cossack* is a 3rd class cruiser of 1770 tons, with an estimated speed of 17 knots; she carries six 6-inch 5-ton guns. Either of these ships would run down a torpedo-boat in anything approaching to a heavy sea.

[10] The staff-commanders of large ships are addressed as "Captain."

[11] The *Victoria* has no protection for her secondary battery against heavy gun fire. This great disadvantage is shared by her sister ship the *Sanspareil*, and by the whole of the ships of the *Admiral* class. The

secondary batteries of the latter are also without protection from machine-gun fire. An attempt has been made to remedy this defect in later ships, such as the *Nile* and *Trafalgar*, by working 4-inch plating on to the sides of the secondary battery.

[12] The Palliser shell are without fuses, and explode on concussion with a hard obstacle such as an armour-plate.

[13] The fact that the *Victoria*, in common with the *Sanspareil*, *Hero*, and *Conqueror*, carries the principal part of her heavy guns forward, constitutes a very serious defect in her design. Actual experience on the *Conqueror* during recent manœuvres confirms the criticism, and the incidents here recounted illustrate it.

[14] It should be remembered that "starboarding" the helm brings the ship's head to port, and *vice versâ*.

[15] The chase is the fore part or muzzle end of a heavy gun. It is clear from the recent experiments that a comparatively slight blow on one of the long, heavy guns now generally in use would disable if not destroy it.

[16] It is evident that either the enemy discharged her torpedo from an above-water port, or that a fragment of a shell had struck the gun-cotton charges below the water-line. The terrible danger attending the use of above-water torpedo ports while under the fire of machine or quick-firing guns is fully appreciated by naval officers, and it is doubtful whether any torpedo would ever be discharged above the water-line in action.

[17] The behaviour of the steel-faced compound armour under repeated blows, as here described, is in accordance with the result of experiments.

[18] There have been several cases of one ironclad being rammed by another; and the result has, as a rule, been as disastrous as that here described. There has not, however, been any case of one very heavy ironclad when running at full speed striking another with the ram. It is possible that the damage to the ramming ship might be greater than here represented. But, judging from the result of a collision which took place between a White Star Liner and an iceberg, it seems fair to assume that the consequences of such collision need not be very serious, or at any rate fatal.

PRINTED BY CASSELL & COMPANY, LIMITED LA BELLE SAUVAGE, LONDON. E.C.
20.691

WORKS BY H. O. ARNOLD-FORSTER.

THE CITIZEN READER. Illustrated. 3 Coloured Plates. 175th Thousand. Price 1s. 6d. With Preface by the late RIGHT HON. W. E. FORSTER, M.P.

"Merely to conceive such a plan was laudable; to carry it out in such a way as to combine interest with instruction is to confer *a national benefit of which it is impossible to exaggerate the value.*"—*Academy.*

"Mr. Arnold-Forster converses with his little readers, and tells them of great things in simple language. He does not alter the facts, nor withhold them. He always remembers that children can see the stars."—*Birmingham Weekly Post.*

MISS CHARLOTTE M. YONGE *says :—*
"Nothing is more wanted than good, cheap papers conveying, not only information on Church matters, but such absolute *simple information on the laws and constitution of the State as is to be found in Mr. Arnold-Forster's admirable 'CITIZEN READER'—a book that should be in every night-school and club-room.*"—*Extract from paper by Miss Yonge, read at Church Congress, October 8th,* 1886.

"It ought to be in use in every English-speaking school in the British Empire."—*Saturday Review.*

"We have no hesitation in pronouncing Messrs. Cassell's 'CITIZEN READER' *the most important contribution to the literature of elementary education that has appeared in the last decade.*"—*Journal of Education.*

"*Every school in the country would be the better for the use and study of this excellent Reader.*"—*The Teachers' Aid.*

"*We feel bound to admit that we know of no school-book of more undoubted practical utility.*"—*The English Teacher.*

"Another plan has just been announced, which has very much to recommend it, and which especially has the virtue of being final. We refer to Mr. Arnold-Forster's paper. . . . We know of no other scheme that is anything like so reasonable and practicable. We cannot doubt that it will receive the most earnest attention of the Government."—*York Herald.*

". . . No real case can be made out against Mr. Arnold-Forster's scheme on grounds of justice."—*Scottish News.*

". . . Mr. Arnold-Forster's scheme deserves examination at length. It is admitted by unfriendly critics to be worthy of attention. Many think it statesmanlike. My advice is, Read it, and then ponder over it. It requires thought, and should not be judged hastily."—*Figaro.*

"Mr. Arnold-Forster proposes to deal with the difficulty in a thorough and novel manner. In his brilliant article he raises the subject from the dead level of disastrous failure, where Mr. Gladstone left it, to the sphere of practical politics. . . ."—*Sheffield Telegraph.*

". . . It offers a solution which is as near finality as anything can well be in this shifting world. . . . We own that we should like to hear what may be urged against the plan, by Irish landlords or tenants, or by economists, or by statisticians, or by objectors on other grounds. At present Mr. Arnold-Forster's case appears to be strong."—*Times.*

"The most noteworthy, perhaps because the boldest, of all the plans for purchasing the land of Ireland from the present proprietors, and making it over to the present tenants, is one described by Mr. Arnold-Forster. It deserves to be known by the name of 'Thorough.' . . ."—*Scotsman.*

". . . Whatever may be thought of its prospects of adoption, it is, at any rate, entitled to the credit of boldness and originality. . . . The process, of course, means perfect justice and complete security to the Irish landlord, and so far, therefore, meets the first requirements of sound legislative principle."—*Observer.*

Works by H. O. Arnold-Forster.

MAP-BUILDING FOR SCHOOLS. A New Method of Instruction in Geography. 6 Maps: England, Scotland, Ireland, France, German Empire, and Europe. 1s. for a Set of 12 Maps.

IN A CONNING TOWER: HOW I TOOK H.M.S. *MAJESTIC* INTO ACTION. Illustrated by MR. W. H. OVEREND. Price 1s.

Ready Shortly.

A NEW and ORIGINAL WORK on GEOGRAPHY. Suitable for use in Schools. Fully Illustrated.

PAUL BERT'S EXPERIMENTAL GEOMETRY. Translated, with Original Examples, by MRS. H. O. ARNOLD-FORSTER. Illustrated. Price 1s. 6d.

From " The Teachers' Aid" :—

"We have been charmed with the perusal of this admirable work. We cannot speak too highly of the benefits accruing from the study of such interesting little treatises as the one before us, and cordially commend it to our readers."

From "Nature" :—

"The book is written in a style that cannot fail to interest children. The illustrations and diagrams are numerous and well-chosen throughout. At the end of the volume exercises have been added for the use of teachers which are not found in the French version.

From " The Scotsman" :—

"The work is written on original lines, and has been excellently translated—a task of no mean difficulty."

CASSELL & COMPANY, LIMITED, *London, Paris & Melbourne.*

CPSIA information can be obtained
at www.ICGtesting.com
Printed in the USA
BVHW040915070223
658044BV00002B/3